DESIGNING YOUR LIFE TO BE WILDLY HAPPY.

“We can either make ourselves miserable, or we make ourselves happy. The amount of work is the same.”

Carlos Castaneda

"Everything is energy and that's all there is to it. Match the frequency of the reality you want and you cannot help but get that reality. It can be no other way. This is not philosophy. This is physics."

Albert Einstein

WELCOME

The idea that I could overcome various 'enemies of creativity' was planted early in my career as a strategist for The Richards Group, an advertising agency in Dallas, TX. They are known for their unorthodox (but brilliant) culture that allows and encourages everyone to 'lose the stuff that isn't important so you can spend time on what is important.' After a few years of letting this philosophy sink in, I moved to Vancouver, BC, which opened my eyes to the philosophy of Feng Shui (the art of placing (and removing) things with intention to bring about desired effects). Once I married these in my mind, I was convinced that I could break out of the conventional thinking that made (most) people less than happy with their everydays. At least less happy than I wanted to be.

The concepts in this book have come from years of searching for and absorbing everything I could find that would help me overcome all the things that drove me nuts. Ruts. Bad Habits. Inefficiency. Because I wanted (and still want) to spend my days (and my life) on things that are way more fun (I'm kind of like that).

I have found that the art of Feng Shui and the Laws of Physics share a key truth: that energy begets like energy. There are levers (people, places, things) that incite positive or negative energy. Our job is to pull it apart so we understand 'what does what' for us and design accordingly. While traditional Feng Shui focuses on one's physical space (furniture and decor), you can (and should) apply this philosophy to every aspect of your life: your finances, time, thoughts, words and actions. This book will show you how.

It is said that we spend more time planning a two-week vacation than we do the course of our lives. I believe that we simply don't know where to start or what tools we have at our disposal. Let me tell you this: you have everything you need right now except a framework to help you clear out the clutter. Revolution is a 10 degree shift, not a 180 degree one. If you do what is asked of you here it will work, even if you don't fully believe in it. Think about it like insurance – it's better to have and not need than need and not have. It simply can't hurt. And it could very well be amazing.

Even one major shift in your thinking can help you reap the rewards of momentum. Momentum is the force that propels us effortlessly toward a desired outcome – getting us farther than conventional (so-called) wisdom would suggest was possible. Think of birds who fly in formation: they draft off each other to save collective energy so they can fly farther than any one would be able to do alone. The ideas in here are birds in your formation. They'll save you from spending time and energy on the things that don't matter so you can spend that time and energy on the things that do.

"Momentum is about harnessing energy."

Lynette Xanders

“The trick is to manage your energy and not just your time.”

Tony Schwartz
(Harvard Business Review)

The framework for this book is based on an algorithm, or a road map if you will, that will provide you with a clear direction for moving forward and creating momentum in your life.

FOCUS + ALIGNMENT + ACTIVATION = MOMENTUM

You have to have a very clear idea of where you're going (focus), then you must cut away all of the sandbags and speed bumps that are in the way of forward progress (alignment). Lastly, you must ignite that which makes your heart sing — your passions — and create forward motion in your actions to create momentum (activation).

To achieve momentum, you need to have all three of these 'plates' spinning. It can be a linear process (start at focus and work your way through) or a non-linear one (begin anywhere that tickles your fancy) but don't avoid a bucket altogether. Usually the one you want to avoid is what you're having the most trouble with and is where you should start, but there's no wrong way in this discovery. Just ask. Be open. And do the work.

This is about making you wildly happy. In order to do this successfully, please don't assume you know what it takes to do that at this moment. Just know that you need momentum that comes from looking at your life creatively (and making resulting decisions) so you can flourish. Creativity is the new wealth. It will get you where you need to go but it often atrophies because of your busy-busy-busy lifestyle. If creativity is a muscle, this book is a personal trainer. Once you know how to make momentum work for you, you can go wherever the wind takes you.

XO

L.

Your path starts here.

"Life is either a daring adventure or nothing at all."

Helen Keller

FO

CUS

Focus may be one of the biggest levers you can apply toward achieving what you wish. If you don't define an ideal situation clearly, you can't work toward that goal. You can't ask for help. You can't incite Providence (see Murray quote at the end). Without focus, you are essentially a ship that isn't moving. Rudderless. Destination-less. Stagnant.

The good news is that you are in charge of setting your course. And if you don't like it, you can reset it. As often as you like.

The only rule of thumb is: do whatever it is you need to do to make you happy. It's not a constant job, just an intensely honest one. I say that because most people avoid thinking about it because it might upset the proverbial apple cart. I submit that if you're reading this, you could use a bit of that. Everything needs to be possible while you consider what you really want and how you really want things to be. But first you have to throw it all up in the air, creating chaos even if only in your mind. The beauty of chaos is that it allows everything to fall back into place the way it should.

It shouldn't be difficult, but it tends to be. You've worked so hard for things to be as they are, you don't want to let go of your current reality even if it isn't working. Again, the good news is that revolution is usually only a 10-degree shift from where you are, not a 180 degree shift.

When my daughter was very young she asked me why I was heading out to do a workshop on a Saturday – what could possibly be so important that I had to do it on a weekend? I explained to her that I was doing a workshop to help people be happier – at work and away from work – and that was a noble goal worthy of my Saturday. She thought for a long time and agreed that it was worthy, but still wondered, "*Why does it take all day?*" Exactly. The best I could come up with was, "That, my dear, is because we have to break the old thinking before we can create new thinking."

Focus is about auditing the levers you have at your disposal so you can start redesigning your life. Knowing what gives you energy and what takes it away is critical. Knowing where you fritter away your time and when you do your best work. And you need to have an intention at the outset of how you want things to be (different). This is your first task. There are some examples in the following exercises that cover a variety of situations (relationships to new job). I know, and you should know, that several of them may not apply to you. So ignore these. Focus on your 'areas of heat' – things you know are a pain point. This work is akin to 'overlapping strokes' so hit the big chunks first across all of the exercises (like skipping stones) before you exhaust yourself trying to make each 'bulletproof perfect.' Awareness is more than half the battle. Don't cramp up before you begin.

DEFINE SUCCESS

Most people answer this question in terms of money. It's perhaps a piece of the puzzle but, overall, I define success very differently. It started with a brain pincher my mom threw my way. When I started making big money, I announced that I wanted an insanely beautiful, sparkly watch. She casually replied, "My definition of success is not having to wear a watch." And then it started. I saw success as freedom and there was no going back. My ideal day would include not having to be anywhere in the morning so I could sleep in (one of my favorite things is to wake up without an alarm) or write (it's when my thoughts are clearest). And there would be no meetings (I later came to redefine meetings as those without food and wine because if you have those things they're conversations, not meetings). This subtle shift (and letting go of the volume of requests) made a massive difference.

What other things define success for me? I wish to eat sushi, play hooky and stay up late watching movies several times a month without worrying about my fiscal balances. I spend time each week doing the things that make my heart sing (even if I don't know how to do them well) like gardening, cooking, riding horses and playing the guitar. I spend time away from work to travel with my family. Some are related to money, but most aren't. Think about how you would spend your time if you were already independently wealthy and start moving that way today.

SUCCESS IS:

What does your ideal state of being look like? It could be about how you spend your time, how you want to feel or what you want to achieve (for example, lazy mornings, no meetings, work out every day, etc.). Write it out or, better yet, find pictures and words and paste them on this page (or someplace else so you can look at it every day).

LIFTS AND DRAINS

Of all the exercises in this book, this may be the most powerful in creating momentum. They're seemingly innocuous questions, centered around things that you don't pay much attention to. But that's the point. These draining people, places and things don't tend to make it into your consciousness because you overlook, ignore or resign yourself to them — 'they're just how things are.' You don't seek these lifts because they're 'not important,' not on your 'to do list' or because you're 'too busy.' This is where you must defy conventional (so-called) wisdom. You must pull apart the details of your life to do more of the good and less of the bad to turn the momentum tide.

It's important to first figure out what the lifts and drains are in your life in order to start realigning your energy. The following exercises involve listing your current inspirations (things that give you energy or improve your mood) as well as your current drains (things that take away your energy or put you in a bad mood) in order to make a few key changes early in the game. The idea is that by increasing a few lifts and removing or reducing a few drains you can create the 'wiggle' needed to recalibrate bigger areas of your life. You must first make space, then manage your energy so you can set off on this adventure in earnest.

“Go confidently in the direction of your dreams. Live the life you have imagined. It’s not what you look at that matters, it’s what you see. Our life is frittered away by detail. Simplify, simplify.”

Henry David Thoreau

WHAT LIFTS YOU UP?

List everything that gives you pleasure, puts a smile on your face or inspires you. This can be a room in your house, a favorite color, an activity, people you know, a place you love to visit, a food — anything that makes you happy. Write down all of the little things because little things are big.

WHAT DRAINS YOUR ENERGY?

List everything that drains your energy, pulls you down or that you try not to think about. Drains can be people (emotional vampires I like to call them), places (think DMV), rooms in the house (especially if there's clutter), thoughts (worries, debt, frustrations, negative mental chatter), things left undone (broken appliances, unwritten letters), or just general, everyday Kryptonite (junk mail, ringing phones, too many emails). Be as specific as you can and list as many as you can. Don't let it get you down – most of these can be resolved to a manageable degree.

TAKE ACTION

Find a way to spend more time doing things that give you energy and make you happy. Go to places that inspire you. Spend time doing things you love. It's easy to fall prey to the 'have to's' that often fill your days (and lives) but there are lots of inexpensive things you can do that will make your heart sing. If you make them a priority, (or really give yourself permission to do them), it will pay off in improved mood and energy. Then you can use this energy to tackle bigger things. This is where creativity comes in — and awareness — to think past the way things are to imagining the way things could be.

On the next page, make a physical note next to each drain with an idea or a solution toward getting rid of that drain. Like most people, you will most likely have large drains you can't immediately fix (like debt), but making a note to tackle it is the first step (and you'll likely feel better just addressing it). You can hire a bookkeeper, get a housekeeper, make an appointment to clean out your closet, gather your receipts, etc. Take a week off of work, spend every Saturday for a month, turn off the TV — whatever it takes. Just make a commitment to get it done — you're worth it.

CHIP AWAY

Write down three things you can do TODAY to remove or reduce any of your drains. DO THEM NOW. For example, trade a chore you hate (with a family member) for one you don't mind doing, set up a smart mailbox to put every email with 'unsubcribe' in it automatically to declutter your inbox, say no or ask for help, throw it out, etc. The first time out, focus on some easy wins then come back to mop up.

SCHEDULE JOY

List all of the little, inexpensive things (walk the dog, take a bath, root around in the garden, color, put fresh flowers in your house, etc.) you can do inside of an hour that will improve your mood or add a little 'play' to your life. Keep this list handy. You need to create a habit of doing more of them.

“We are what we think, all that we are arises with our thoughts. With our thoughts, we make the world.”

Buddha

CATEGORIZE YOUR ACTIONS

Audit how you spend your time. Not just the big chunks of time (sleeping, eating, working), but the little chunks of time (checking email, watching TV) and the little niblets of time (thinking of what to make for dinner, looking for things, etc.). You want to steal the time you spend on unimportant things in order to fill your bank of time to spend on important things.

Here's a useful framework for evaluating how you spend your time (from Stephen Covey); put all of your activities into four quadrants:

1. Important and urgent (like feeding the kids)
2. Unimportant but seemingly urgent (email, texts)
3. Important but not urgent (time for you)
4. Unimportant and not urgent (junk mail, TV)

Hack away at the unimportant areas. Make things feel less urgent. For instance, turn off the electronic bells — a ringing phone is an invitation, not a command, and if you get to your email an hour later, the sky won't fall.

Spend your time on the things that are most important in reality, (like time for you, your creativity, lifts), not how they appear or how much they demand your attention. If you find you can 'steal time' from unimportant quadrants, you've just found more wiggle. You're driving. Where do you want to go?

"What do you want to have happen? How will you know when you get there?"

FEEL YOUR WAY

We often live in our heads and get stuck because it conflicts with what we know in our hearts (and guts). And we usually want to jump to the end – to know what the tactic is that will get us somewhere else – without letting the thinking wash over us in order to let our intuition guide us. This can lead to a lot of false starts and lost momentum. First we must learn to pay attention to how things *feel*.

Don't assume you know what the answer looks like. You need to observe, then ask. For example, walking into a beautiful hotel lobby feels a bit different than walking into the DMV. If you acknowledge how this affects you physically and put into words how each feels, you're more likely to be able to navigate the world, collecting more of the things that make you feel alive and fewer of the things that make you feel exhausted.

Start thinking about things a little differently than you might have before. Pay attention. Put into words what you're looking for in terms of how you want to feel (secure? electrified? powerful?).

DEFINE THE FEELING

How do you want to feel that's different from how you feel now?

WRITE A BRIEF

Writing a brief (or in this case, creating a finite list defined by a clear intention) is putting down on paper what you want more of so you can better grasp what your heart and not your head, needs or wants. I know what you're thinking — why do I need to write this down? Because you need to unpack what success looks like. Unpacking it and putting words to it is what gives it power. You often won't know what you think or want until it comes out in words. And the Universe cannot conspire to help you get what you want if you aren't focused on what you want.

I once had to call an animal behaviorist because my Newfie was driving me nuts. He (the behaviorist) asked me what her (the Newfie's) job was. I had no idea. I supposed I wanted her to lie at my feet quietly while I worked. It hadn't occurred to me to define this beyond 'stop driving me nuts' until this point. He said I should expect more. Define it. And then ask for it. He was right. Unpacking what success looks like for us in relation to what we want from others at different times helps us collectively dance through the day, instead of wrestle, because we're trying to read minds.

Here's another example: I ask people to write down the 10 things they want in a partner, they automatically list things like "must be tall, have a good job, etc." That's jumping to the end. What they should focus on is how they might spend time together or what shared traits would create the most harmony in everyday situations. For example, 'must love dogs, must sleep in, must ride roller coasters and believe in magic.' If they end up being tall with a good job all the better, but I promise you the latter will make you happier than the former.

ASK FOR LOVE

When do you feel the most loved? What experiences that you adore are even better shared? Write a brief for the partner you desire:

ASK FOR A JOB

What types of people inspire you to do your best work? What does your happy workplace look like? What motivates you? What do you love about your craft? Write a brief for the perfect 'job':

“If this isn’t great, what is? And if not now, when?”

Paraphrase from Kurt Vonnegut

AM I ASKING FOR TOO MUCH?

This question was posed by a woman who was writing a brief for love by unpacking all she'd learned about what worked and didn't work for her from previous relationships. This is big. I don't believe there's such a thing as asking for too much (although you do only get 10 things, so more than this perhaps tips the scale), but in terms of scope, want what you want. Own it. In effect, this defines your self-worth.

What do you think you deserve? I think it aligns well with the advice I got when I left my agency to go freelance: "If your toes don't curl, you're not asking for enough [money]." The same applies here. Ask for what you really want. Try it on like a coat for a day. Revise if you need to. But be true to yourself and don't settle even before you've become aware of what it might look like (on paper). The following quote encapsulates this idea much more eloquently and brings to life the idea of getting exactly what you intend. Repeat the last two lines out loud. Rinse. Repeat.

"I bargained with Life for a penny,
And Life would pay no more,
However I begged at evening
When I counted my scanty store;

For Life is just an employer,
He gives you what you ask,
But once you have set the wages,
Why you must bear the task.

I worked for a menial's hire,
Only to learn, dismayed,
That any wage I had asked of Life,
Life would have willingly paid."

Napoleon Hill

LEARN THE ART OF ASKING

From all the CEO success stories I've studied, they seem to agree on one thing: that the greatest indicator of whether a person will be successful or not in business (and in life) is directly related to their ability to ask for help. Full stop. And all you really need to say is 'yes, please' and 'thank you.' I hear many people say 'no' as fast as it can come out of their mouths when someone offers to help them – often before they've even considered whether they need the help or not. Think about when you're asked at a check-out line if you need help out with your groceries – it doesn't happen often, but still – it's an automated response, isn't it? What you're thinking is, 'I don't want you go to the trouble' or 'I am fully capable,' but that's not the point. And you don't need a long explanation or excuse. Consider that it's a gift to someone else to allow them to help you – especially if they've offered.

Practice saying these phrases out loud and looking for things to ask people to help you with. Refer to your 'When you feel the most loved' list, or your drains list, and articulate what you would love someone else to do for you to make you even happier. If you're stuck, refer to the "Things Others Could do to Make me Happier" list that follows.

YES, PLEASE...

Write down your top three greatest requests of others; then actually ask for them! You'll be amazed at what magic ensues.

"If you don't ask, you don't get."

Lynette's Dad

THINGS OTHERS COULD DO TO MAKE ME HAPPIER*...

- ☐ Change your underwear
- ☐ Tell me I'm smart
- ☐ Stop sulking
- ☐ Vote often
- ☐ Get better mileage
- ☐ Convert
- ☐ Bend over
- ☐ Go to the store
- ☐ Project confidence
- ☐ Blow your nose
- ☐ Try harder
- ☐ Stop scratching
- ☐ Fluff the pillows
- ☐ Watch the road
- ☐ Give back my pen
- ☐ Use punctuation
- ☐ Learn CPR
- ☐ Shiver me timbers
- ☐ Smile
- ☐ Tell me the truth
- ☐ Save me a seat
- ☐ Get off your high horse
- ☐ Wash away the gray
- ☐ Care
- ☐ Do what I say
- ☐ Keep your voice down
- ☐ Be there for me
- ☐ Redecorate
- ☐ Tolerate my family
- ☐ Eat brussel sprouts
- ☐ Take a deep breath
- ☐ Hire a personal trainer
- ☐ Cheer up
- ☐ Judge not
- ☐ Admire my ass
- ☐ Take me off your list
- ☐ Stand up for yourself
- ☐ Change faster
- ☐ Answer the phone
- ☐ Smile and nod
- ☐ Feign Jealousy
- ☐ Let me sleep in
- ☐ Spend more
- ☐ Float my boat
- ☐ Rewind
- ☐ Stop that
- ☐ Pass the salt
- ☐ Pluck
- ☐ Stop calling me that
- ☐ Call me back
- ☐ Soar with the eagles
- ☐ Count your carbs
- ☐ Stop counting my carbs
- ☐ Be attractive to others
- ☐ Change the channel
- ☐ Prepare for the worst
- ☐ Walk the cat
- ☐ Walk on water
- ☐ Drive a stick
- ☐ Lie to me
- ☐ Dream a little dream
- ☐ Fix it
- ☐ Believe in magic

*Modified from a list I found on Knockknock.biz.

- ☐ Wave goodbye
- ☐ Eat shellfish
- ☐ Turn off the alarm
- ☐ Practice oral hygiene
- ☐ Get your hands off me
- ☐ Take me somewhere
- ☐ Taste rain
- ☐ Fill the tank
- ☐ Make the reservation
- ☐ Take up a trade
- ☐ Drop your attitude
- ☐ Renounce desire
- ☐ Matter
- ☐ Grow it out
- ☐ Sit still
- ☐ Force the issue
- ☐ Appease me
- ☐ Stuff your face
- ☐ Say "excuse me"
- ☐ Get rid of your junk
- ☐ Unplug
- ☐ Let me finish
- ☐ Use crosswalks
- ☐ Turn me to jelly
- ☐ Love my dog
- ☐ Ride roller coasters
- ☐ Deal with it
- ☐ Live a little
- ☐ Take my side
- ☐ Pray
- ☐ Turn off the light
- ☐ Steal a kiss
- ☐ Open your mind
- ☐ Explain it for me
- ☐ Back up your hard drive
- ☐ Manage healthcare
- ☐ Make lasagna
- ☐ Get that mole removed
- ☐ Motivate me
- ☐ Put the cereal away
- ☐ Surprise me
- ☐ Be aggressive
- ☐ Be passive
- ☐ Do your own laundry
- ☐ Sprinkle it with sunshine
- ☐ Write it down
- ☐ Hold me
- ☐ Flirt with me
- ☐ Live long and prosper
- ☐ Shave
- ☐ Make it up to me
- ☐ Don't let go
- ☐ Curl my toes
- ☐ Take it outside
- ☐ Trust me
- ☐ Change your ringtone
- ☐ Do it faster
- ☐ Rub harder
- ☐ Pick off the pepperoni
- ☐ Don't smoke
- ☐ Cover your eyes
- ☐ Learn a new trick
- ☐ Relocate
- ☐ Pretend you're listening
- ☐ Get on the bus
- ☐ Be my alibi
- ☐ Increase my joy
- ☐ Eat your dinner
- ☐ Cut your toenails
- ☐ Count to ten
- ☐ Come home
- ☐ Amplify
- ☐ Slow down
- ☐ Love me forever
- ☐ Never say never
- ☐ Watch my show with me
- ☐ Go commando
- ☐ Tell me a joke

SET FLYWHEEL GOALS

Now that you've got the hang of it, make sure you're addressing your entire 'flywheel.' As my dad explained it to me, think of your life as a flywheel (the part inside a gyroscope that looks like a spaceship — or think of a spinning plate if that works). The idea is that it is in motion clockwise or counterclockwise. But it can also be tilted so that one side is higher and another lower — it's no longer 'flying' straight. It wobbles. And that wobble creates more wobble until it stops spinning. The way to keep your flywheel flying straight is to make sure you're not overemphasizing some things at the expense of others.

Some people think of goals in terms of money or career. For others, their life goals focus around health or losing weight. The focus is different for different people and that's fine. Whatever moves you is important to keep. This exercise, however, is about making sure you have other important aspects of your life covered. Do you have career/money goals? Health/fitness goals? Relationship goals? What about creativity goals? Mental health? Parenting? The key is to put into words what you want to be different across all aspects of your life, not just the ones that are nagging at you right now.

Here's what my flywheel looks like:

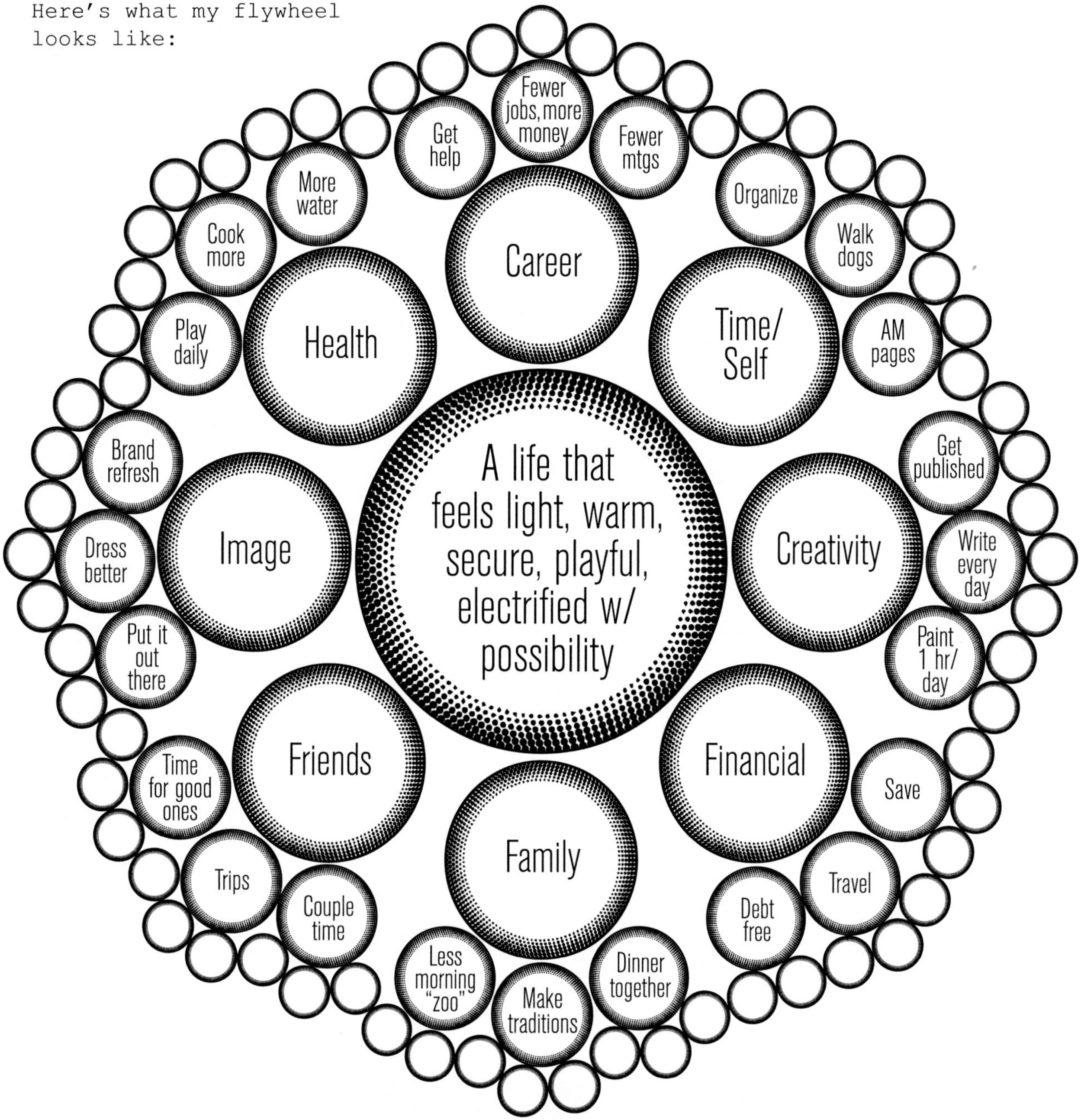

WRITE THEM DOWN

There's a lovely story in the book, *Creating Wealth,* about a study that was done with a graduating class at an Ivy League college to assess the impact of writing down financial goals. The research measured students who did and didn't have financial goals, and how many of them wrote those goals down. They went back years later to the same people to find out if anything different happened to those who had financial goals vs. those who didn't and those who wrote them down vs. those who didn't. The findings uncovered an amazing result: The 10% who had goals but didn't write them down were no different than those without goals. However, the 3% who WROTE DOWN their financial goals made more money than the other 97% combined. They attributed that difference to nothing other than the fact that they wrote down their goals. Writing it down is an ACTION and it 'speaks' much louder than words, right?

This does not apply only to financial goals, obviously, but to everything we've been talking about to this point. Writing down things you don't need to remember gets them out of your head. Writing down things you're mulling over will keep them from flying around your head and driving you crazy. If you're writing negative stuff to get it out, burn it. But the most important thing is to put words and numbers to what you want more of. Writing is power.

BE REALLY SPECIFIC

In the land of 'be careful what you wish for,' I want to caution you to be very specific and focus on how you want to feel when you achieve your goal as opposed to what tactic you think will help you achieve your goal. Many goal books will tell you that specifics are much more powerful. General is 'I want to lose weight,' specific is 'I want to lose eight pounds,' ideal is 'I want to feel amazing in good clothes' (an outcome of losing eight pounds). If you want to feel rich or unstressed about money, put a number to what will make you feel secure/wildly happy. Put a number to how many weeks of vacation you want. Remember, you want to measure impact and you can't do that if you don't have a baseline and a specific goal.

One of my favorite little anecdotes around the downside of not being utterly specific is from Tammy Faye Baker. Really. She said in one of her last interviews that when she was a little girl she used to "pray and pray and pray...God, please make my life interesting...I realized too late that I should have been MUCH more specific."

WHAT ARE YOUR SHORT-TERM GOALS?

WHAT ARE YOUR LONG-TERM GOALS?

Fill out your flywheel:

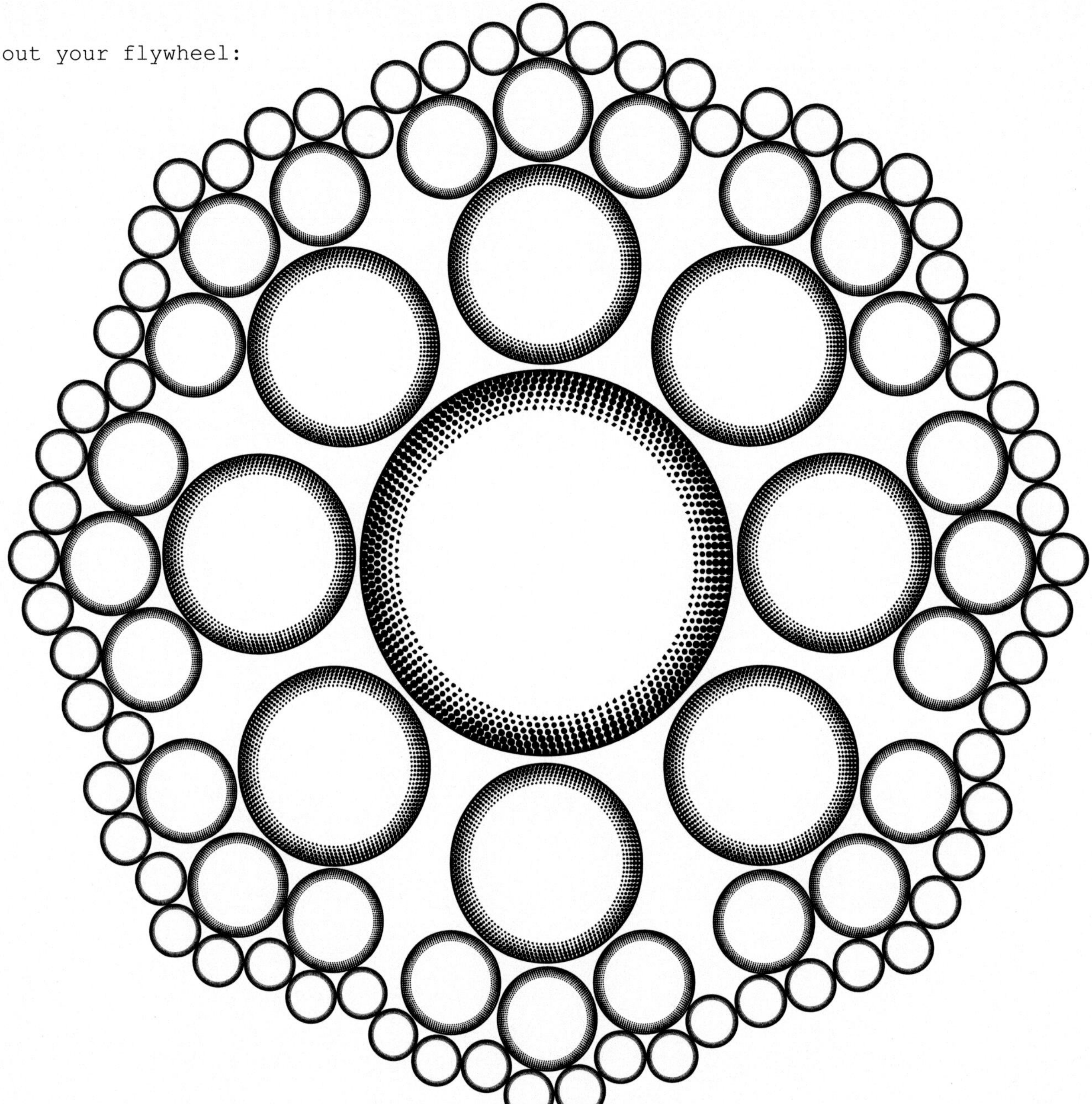

WHAT DID YOU MISS?

OVERCOME FEAR

Not having a clear vision of success is the greatest enemy to achieving success. The second, I believe, is being afraid. Fear is amplified in your brain. If you put words to your fears, you often find they're not as big and scary and unwieldy as you might have thought. You need to train yourself to overcome fear by cultivating courage. It's a muscle, similar to creativity. You call on it. You build it or let it atrophy. There are a few different ways you can build it depending upon what you're most afraid of.

I was terrified of going freelance, but I was miserable not working for myself. So I decided to face my fears by writing down/laddering up my fears. What if no one hired me? What if I wasn't able to feed myself? What if I became homeless? All valid fears. I couldn't just forget they were there. But I could find a safety net or what I call a 'rockin' plan b.' I decided that if I owned my home, I could never become homeless. But it would take me years to pay off a house, so I considered, 'what about a condo? A cabin?' I began to redefine home. What did I really need to cover 'home?' I needed to be able to fit into it with my Newfie and some stuff I loved. And I had to be able to lock it. This was the essential list. And then I realized I could be just as easily describing an SUV. If I owned a truck outright that was big enough for me and my dog, I would never be homeless.

I asked an auto broker for 10 things I wanted in this truck. He told me he'd never seen a car like that come across his desk in 10 years but he'd look anyway. When he called two days later, he was nearly speechless. A perfect match showed up. I wrote a check and went freelance the next day. I'm happy to say I've never had to sleep in my truck but I have, to this day, a 'pack for evacuation vehicle' that is bigger (because I have a kid and a husband and three animals to fit into it now), if I need it. And it still helps me to sleep well at night. It may be different for you, but the concept is the same. Name it and then work around it.

"If you have a rockin' plan b, nothing truly bad can happen."

Lynette Xanders

WHAT IS THE WORST THAT CAN HAPPEN AND WHAT COULD BUFFER YOU FROM IT?

“Remember that fear and exhilaration feel exactly the same. Learn to love it.”

Lynette Xanders

EMBRACE YOUR FEARS

The other way I keep my fears at bay is to recalibrate the truth of success. I study 'so-called' failures. To combat the fear of rejection, I remember that publishers rejected and sent back *Lord of the Flies* to the author, William Golding, 21 times.

If it's fear of failure, I think about Michael Jordan not making the basketball team in high school or Einstein failing algebra (this actually tells me more about high school, but that's a separate topic).

If I'm bummed that music isn't playing for others when I know I have a good idea, I think about the concept for FedEx that received a 'C' at HBS because it was a flawed concept (even if this turns out to be a myth, it still helps me).

If I need to build up my resistance to feeling terrified, I ride roller coasters until that feeling subsides. It's like building up a callous in order to keep myself from hyperventilating.

Most of all, I remember that fear and exhilaration feel exactly the same. And to have a rich life, I need to decide that I love that feeling. If you can't change something, change how you feel about it. It's a requirement for me so that I can do more than push papers around until the day that I can, hopefully, retire. None of it comes easily because it's scary. But nothing I worried about at any stage actually happened. And I hate wasting a good worry.

WHAT CAN YOU DO TODAY TO CULTIVATE COURAGE?

"Sometimes you just gotta say, 'What the fuck.'"

Risky Business

HAPPINESS IS A CHOICE.

CHANGE IT OR CHANGE HOW YOU FEEL ABOUT IT.

ALIGN

MENT

Alignment is a continual process of refinement. It won't get done in one 'stroke of the brush' – it's more like overlapping strokes. The early speed bumps will fall away and you'll breeze over them in review, running up against the next thing in line to tackle.

The basic idea of alignment is to 'lose all that does not serve you.' With that in mind, the first step is to audit what's working for you and what isn't. That includes what's in your head, how you spend your time, and the people, places and things that surround you.

As with focus, the magic of proper alignment is to feel your way through as opposed to thinking your way through. Look around and pay attention to how things make you feel. Do certain things bring you joy? Do certain things make you feel exhausted? Revisit your lifts and drains. Make sure you have a list of everything that inspires you, makes your heart sing, lifts you up, gives you momentum and all those things that bring you down. Don't think someone else can give you this list. Clutter is a common drain, but there will be a great many things that are unique to you. This list should be more about things you can control (certain chores, for example) and not about things outside of your control (like war).

Recognize the power of resistance in this process – the universal conspiracy to keep things the way they are. You need to begin to build a muscle for creating the right habits and the right kind of thinking, and lose the bad habits and the bad thinking (they are inextricably intertwined). And we will tackle resistance together.

"We cannot solve our problems with the same level of thinking that created them."

Albert Einstein

EMBRACE CHAOS

The greatest enemy to tackle when making any kind of change is resistance. Our own personal resistance comes from the desire to not undo what has been done (even if it's not working for us). The other kind of resistance is the larger breed: the universal conspiracy to keep things the way they are (read more in Steven Pressfield's *War of Art*). We'll tackle ways to break up external resistance in the Activation section, but it's important that you get past your own resistance in order to fully embrace the art of alignment.

The way to blow up your internal resistance is to embrace chaos. Accept that things must be undone in order to reorganize. Think about cleaning a closet. You have to take it all out — see it as it is in context — and then start culling. It looks worse for a short time before it starts looking better. Getting to this point can be tricky but it helps to write down what you want to see change or, in other words, how things could be better. Once you fall in love with how things could be you're more apt to let go of how things are. This is likely a life-long process, but at this point you have to embrace the new and the unknown, even if only on a small scale, to get comfortable with chaos.

“One must still have chaos in oneself to give birth to a dancing star.”

Friedrich Nietzsche

HOW COULD THINGS BE BETTER?

Write down things you want to change (could be as simple as cleaning out your garage or as big as getting out of a negative relationship). Don't worry about whether or not you think it's possible.

TWO THINGS

Now take a look at your list — what two decisions, if you make them right now, will change your life for the better?

“One’s life shrinks and expands in proportion to One’s courage.”

Anäis Nin

I CHING

If you are having a hard time making this decision, here's a lovely little way to force a decision and learn how to recognize your intuitive voice. Pendulums are sold in many New Age stores that can SHOW you how you feel about something (by reading your energy), but here's a quick, easy way to do it anytime, anywhere:

1. Collect three coins. If you're going for extra credit, find three that have dates that mean something to you — but it'll work regardless (read through these instructions first, then do it).

2. You need to have a 'yes' or 'no' question in your mind. Then you'll hold the coins in your hand and breathe on them before asking your (one) question. You'll throw the pennies on a tabletop to get your 'answer.' All heads is 'yes.' All tails is 'no.' A mix means it's leaning in a direction. Now that you're set up, ask and throw.

3. The key is to pay attention to how you feel about the answer. If you're relieved (regardless of the 'answer'), you have your answer. If you want to throw them again, ta da! Same deal.

PRACTICE THE ART OF JOURNALING

One of the best habits to embrace early on is journaling. Yes, really. It's an activity that has gotten a bad reputation — mostly because people tend to only journal about the bad stuff. I want you to put on your positive hat when you start journaling; whatever you write down gives it power. It amplifies it. It is a wish or an 'ask' for more of the same. So keep it positive and only write down the good stuff. This kind of journaling is intended to capture the thoughts and feelings that don't get your attention any other way. It's a way for your subconscious to speak to you. The magic is in putting thoughts and feelings into words. Writing them down brings a special sauce to the process that I can't fully explain, but totally believe in.

It doesn't have to be forever — about 21 days — until you've established some new habits and new thoughts that will sustain your momentum toward your new life. Get a book with blank pages. Fill it with things that speak to you, provoke you, inspire you. Doodle in it. Keep track of ideas, great quotes, questions, observations. Write about accomplishments. Dreams. Things you are grateful for. People you admire. Places you want to travel to. Definitely keep track of your mantras and goals and definitions of success. Make it a lightning rod for everything you think is amazing in this world. Give your positive, creative thoughts a place to land and you'll open the floodgates to channeling more of them.

"Putting things to words is powerful. Writing these words down straps a rocket to them and sends your wishes straight to the ears of the Universe."

Lynette Xanders

Practice Morning Pages

This is from Julia Cameron's *The Artist's Way*. It is a fabulous habit to cultivate (that I pull out periodically whenever I'm stuck or feel agitated but can't quite figure out why). The trick is to write three pages first thing in the morning (before your internal editor has woken up). It can be a general brain dump just to 'clear your ram,' you can write about something specific or answer 'hot' questions. Make it a habit to at least turn to this ritual when you're feeling stuck.

Incite Pavlov

Starting a ritual around writing will tap your subconscious and get you into the right head space. Creating rituals 'pre-heats' your brain to know what is going to be asked of it before it is asked. This helps you get to the brain space you need to tap faster. I'm a fan of lighting a candle and playing the same playlist (I like songs without words or in a language I don't speak so I'm not fully distracted but have distracted my distract-able mind). When these external cues are tapped, Pavlov kicks in (subconscious associations) and we're prepped for the task. Most über-rich have morning rituals most likely to save energy and prep for more important things.

Look for ways to create associations and rituals around focused time. This can be when you want to think/write, when you need to work, when you and your significant other are working on your finances or planning for the future, when you want to work out. Whatever you can do to 'set the stage' for these various activities, the more likely you will actually do them (and do them faster/more easily). Easy is better.

RITUALS

List some things you can do that could turn into a ritual and get your juices flowing:

WHAT ARE YOUR HOT QUESTIONS?

I like to keep a list of 'hot' questions because identifying the problem is more than half the battle. I find the key is to take a stab at answering the tough questions. List a few things to ponder: What if . . . ? Why not . . . ?

Focus on the Positive

Most of us have the tendency to write about the negative — and we have to build the habit of not griping. The unfortunate rule of thumb is that we need to hear a compliment 10 times before it sinks in but we'll remember a slag forever even if we only hear it once. Negative is easier. Negative lingers. We have to fight hard to bring forward the positive in our thoughts and in our words.

Exercise this muscle by writing about positive things: 100 things you love about yourself, the best compliments you've ever received, 10 things you're grateful for, etc. At the end of each day, list all the good that happened. The more you focus on the positive, the more easily you'll see the positive (which can really change your attitude).

You really do get more of what you focus on. It's that old law of attraction at work. And if you think that it's a New Age-y pile, consider that it's a Law of Physics (energy begets like energy). What you put out you get back. Make your words, thoughts and attention focus on the positive and it'll buoy everything.

WHAT GOOD HAPPENED TODAY?

List all of the little things that went more easily than you thought, made you feel good, etc.:

WHAT ARE YOU GRATEFUL FOR? PROUD OF?

Write down 10 things for each:

Really Answer

Over time, many people are able to stem negativity (it'll back off once you stop giving it power), and some have good luck noticing the positive. What falls through the cracks tend to be those thoughts that are benign on the surface – things we think or say in broad strokes without unpacking them. My advice is to work hard to put words to thoughts and feelings. Especially those you think you know inherently but live in that vague, ungrounded ether of your mind. When you see a blue crayon, do you only think blue? Or do you think robin's egg, cobalt, cornflower, Windsor, etc.? In order to have access to all of the levers you can affect, you need to be aware of how you react to things, how you view things and how you *describe things*.

Given that it must not be easy living with me, I've required my daughter to put words to things like 'tell me all the good things that happened today' instead of 'how was your day?' When she was little we went skiing in Sun Valley and she said, "Wow, this is a nice place." Since she was only about three and a half, I asked her to tell me how she knew it was a nice place. After a few "I don't know's," she said, "because it's beautiful everywhere you look." That's a rockin' answer. And now she knows how she defines a "nice place."

DESCRIBE IT RICHLY

Practice putting words to things you know (like explaining the glory of a hot bath after a day of skiing or how ice cream on a hot day makes you feel).

PRACTICE MIS-EN-PLACE

This is the beginning stage of getting past resistance and fueling momentum. Most people who are stuck have a great deal of clutter (we'll tackle that when we get there). This element is taking a small piece of the madness and putting order to it. You're going to start with skipping stones across a variety of areas of clutter to get the wheels turning.

Mis-en-place is a philosophy among French Chefs (and Tim Ferris) of 'putting everything in its place' prior to diving into a creative endeavor, whether cooking or creating a business. For instance, when you're cooking you would cut and measure your ingredients and set up your pans/ appliances before you turn on the heat. The result is better work with less stress, less drama and fewer flaming mistakes.

It's about clearing your space and clearing your mind in order to set yourself up to do your best work. It can be a ritual, but it can also be an efficiency driver, which is a double whammy.

Part of the benefit of this approach is obvious: it saves you time looking for things (you can't take over the world if you can't find your keys kind-of-thing), but it's more than that. It's the equivalent of 'clearing the cache' in your mental computer. Saving valuable RAM for processing. In essence, it's clearing the clutter that creates resistance and breaking up the speed bumps that prevent the flow of energy (that is creativity and productivity).

It's a war on clutter of every kind. Clutter feeds resistance. Killing it will feed you. Here's a quick list of big impact actions to eliminate clutter and prep for creative endeavors (or sanity):

Deep physical cleaning. This includes: Clearing off your computer desktop, clearing out your email, clearing off, organizing and wiping down your physical desktop, knowing where your money is going, knowing where to find your important papers, getting up-to-date on all your doctor's appointments (and vet) and cleaning out your fridge. The best rule of thumb when tackling these jobs is to put like things together and lose all that does not serve you.

Deep mental clearing. This includes getting rid of the floating bits in your head (write down lists or things you're trying to remember or just let them go entirely).

Daily mental cleaning. I usually don't have the mental energy to think or write past 3 pm, but my organizing abilities are working just fine, so I start prepping for my next day. This includes: printing all docs for meetings, putting addresses into my maps app, confirming lunch dates or prepping my lunch, picking out my clothes, filling the gas tank and cleaning out my wallet. All of this before I go to bed! This allows me to hit the ground running and avoid land mines that create drama so I can spend my energy creating something amazing.

AUDIT YOUR TIME AND ENERGY

We are creatures that have a great capacity to ignore things. This includes keeping track of 'what's happened.' We focus on what we have left to do and not on what we've done. The way to change this is to first track, second record and finally evaluate what you do each day so you can look at it objectively — and bring to the forefront things you ignore or gloss over.

A study was done with CEO's that illustrates this point beautifully. Several CEO's were asked to write down, from memory, how they spent their time during a typical day. Then these CEO's were shadowed to see how much overlap there was in how they actually spent their time. In short, VERY little overlap. This exercise made them see how they completely forgot about all the little things that sucked up their days (HR issues, IT issues, etc.). Their mental did not match their actual. This is what you want to get to.

I touched on this subject earlier when I asked you to categorize your actions. This was necessary to create wiggle early on, but now it's time for a deeper dive with an eye to the actual.

TRACK IT

For one week, capture everything you spend time doing. At the end of the week, tally the time spent on each major activity (eating, shopping, checking email, driving, etc.) and capture as many of the little things as possible. Take a deep breath...no wonder you're so tired!

DESIGN AN IDEAL DAY

The end goal of this exercise is to draw two pie charts — one that illustrates everything you spend time on in a typical day (in respective portions of 24 hours) and one that reflects a more ideal day.

This can reveal some insights around how you define success as well as show you some baby steps for moving toward it. Most people spend their time sleeping, working, dealing with food (shopping, cooking, eating, cleaning up) and grooming. Pay attention to the little bits between these elements (as well as how you can be more efficient in these activities to give you more time for other things that you often 'don't have enough time' to do).

Here's an example: D worked for an amazing agency and was fairly happy with her life with two exceptions (that she wasn't fully aware of until she did this exercise). When she focused on her activities, D found she was frustrated with two things: she didn't have 'down' time to watch TV because she spent that time also doing chores, which resulted in not being terribly efficient at completing her chores and not terribly satisfied with her TV watching time. Her other point of frustration was that she couldn't seem to carve out time to work on her freelance projects. When she looked at her wheel, she had a two-hour block of time that was labeled "waiting" — she ended up waiting for her husband during this time because they carpooled and had no set schedule for heading home.

So they agreed that he would not pick her up until 7 pm every night, which left her time to work on her freelance projects. She also decided to complete her chores as soon as she got home and then watch TV uninterrupted as a reward. Tiny changes, big effects.

Another example: L. wanted to tweak small things at work. She cleaned her office and bought her favorite flowers for her desk, but she still felt a bit trapped. She was so rushed in the mornings taking her daughter to school it set a bad tone for the rest of the day. She decided to ask her boss if she could come in a bit later in the morning and be trusted to make up for it elsewhere — essentially being judged on her outputs and not the amount of time at her desk — and he agreed. When she made a few small changes within her control, she realized that something else was still bugging her. This provided her with the momentum to ask others for what she needed. It took less than a week to change her world.

Being aware allows you to recalibrate your time and energy. Find what serves you, lose what doesn't serve you and identify what needs to change to make your every day better. It sounds unrealistically simple, but in my experience it's way simpler and easier than most people ever imagine. First you have to be aware (clear), then you must ask and then act. Redesign with intention.

Your Typical Day

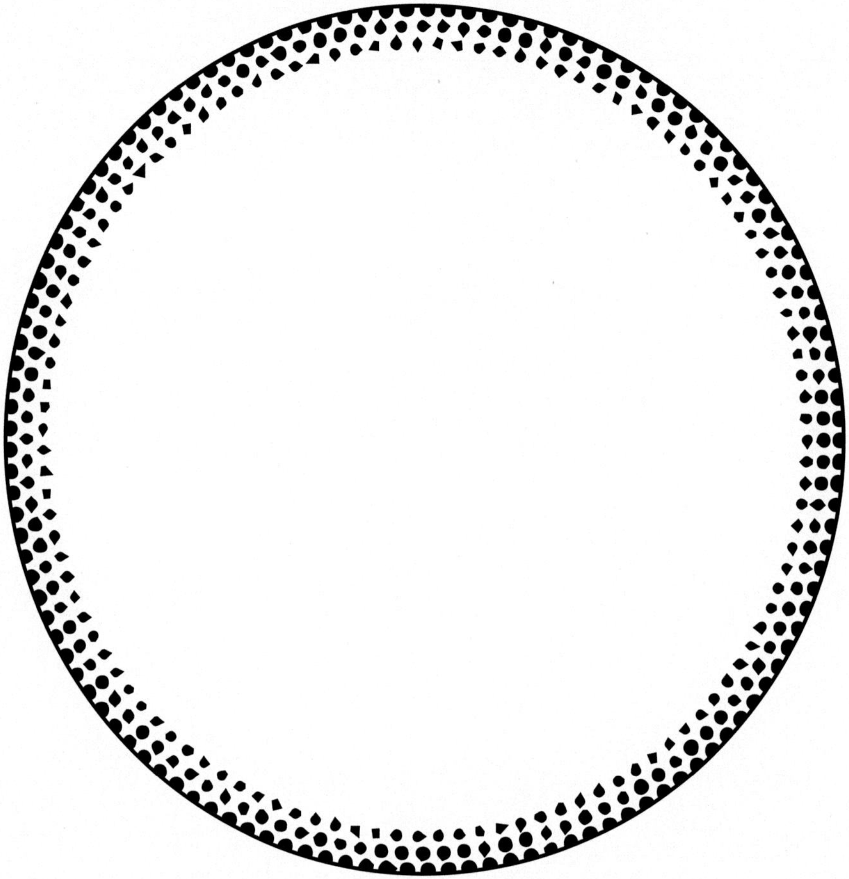

What can you trade or reallocate to get here?

Your Ideal Day

DEFRAG THE CALENDAR

Another giant enemy of momentum (and creativity) is fragmentation (aka distraction) especially when it relates to how you do your best work in the course of a day.

Bundle your 'to do's' in terms of where you are — driving, at work, at your computer, etc. Then audit when you do your best work (including what type of work) and schedule your days accordingly. For example, I do my best thinking and writing in the morning — which surprises me because I'm not technically a morning person — because my critical editor hasn't woken up yet. I'm groggy enough to let it flow and fresh enough to be excited. If, instead, I spend my morning answering emails, I've wasted that ideal time (and energy).

Think about this: If you are on an airplane, you usually can't answer emails for a few hours and the sky doesn't fall. You have to give yourself permission to pretend you're on an airplane so you can take a morning or a half day to think and write. Start with the hardest thing first. Then you can schedule a different day (ideally) or time of day to meet/talk/travel. Mixing the two requires you to piece-meal your attention, which isn't ideal for productivity or creativity. Then, instead of focusing on what you have scheduled for the day, start looking for the time between things as opportunities to get items off your to-do list so that you have bigger blocks of time for the important things. Essentially, you are designing your day around what works best for your rhythm.

WHEN DO YOU DO YOUR BEST WORK?

Look at your schedule and pay attention to what you feel like doing. Make notes about when you are the most productive and when you are the most creative. How would you design your days so you are doing your best work?

MAKE SPACE

You're not only reducing the unwelcome kind of chaos here (drama from being late), you're demonstrating an intention (the strongest kind of 'ask') with this one. Some might seem impossible but I assure you, they are likely only a bit inconvenient. And only really at first.

Schedule 10-30 minutes between meetings to avoid the mad dash/running late. Don't actually take notes in meetings, but spend the time thinking and talking and write down next steps at the end (instead of thinking you're going to do the thinking later).

The second kind of 'make space' is to create a space in your home for creativity. We tend to spend the majority of our time doing things that miraculously correlate with the biggest rooms in our house. If we have a space for something, we're more likely to find ourselves there doing that thing (exercise equipment is a frequent exception but I think it's because they tend to make such great clothes hangers).

Where would the most creative space in your home be? For many, it's a home office that's full of storage, which is not de-cluttered and is usually not inspiring. And it needs to be to fuel your creative self. Create a space to house things that speak to your passions, whether it's photos, quotes, books or crayons. Making a space for creativity (the best precursor to good work and good play) is one of the biggest forms of 'mis-en-place.'

DESIGN A SHRINE

Identify possible creative spaces in your home. If you only have a closet or a corner of a room, create a 'shrine' to your passions. List out things you could put there that would inspire you:

WATCH FOR SPACES

It's about retraining yourself to see what you've previously ignored. My favorite analogy is what skiers in trees and motorcyclists in traffic have to learn to avoid serious injury. Novices will look at the obstacle and think "don't hit the tree, don't hit the tree, don't hit the tree." But the mind doesn't pay much attention to the negative in that thought. It hears, "tree, tree, tree" and, inevitably, that is where you will head. To keep from having that pine fresh scent all day, you have to retrain yourself to SEE THE SPACES and actively make yourself aware of them, by looking for and noticing 'space, space, space.'

Start looking for spaces in your schedule (time between meetings, early mornings) and in your down time (if I combine X and Y, I will have time for Z). Once you start looking at spaces and not events, you'll see more room for opportunity.

"Do or do not, there is no try."

Yoda

“The music is not in the notes, but in the silence in between.”

Wolfgang Amadeus Mozart

ACTIV

ATION

Activation is the proverbial juice that gets the ship moving. I think of it as action, movement, perhaps even electricity, that comes from change, efficiency, focus and doing the things you love.

By now you've touched the very tip of the momentum you can get from organizing, clearing clutter, losing drains and setting out an intention. Now you're going to jump into the master class. You are going to address the people, places and things you can affect that will supercharge your flow, your momentum, your creativity and your happiness.

You are a rocket ship, ready to take off. Think about this: in its travel to outer space, a rocket contains thousands of gallons of fuel. You might think that it would require half its fuel to get half way – or perhaps to get there – and the other half to get back. The reality is that the amount of resistance to keep it in our atmosphere is so strong that a rocket uses *half* of its total fuel just to get past the *first mile* of atmosphere after takeoff. Momentum is what carries the rocket forward once propulsion is created to the tune of *there and back on half a tank*. That means the changes you're making now are much harder then they will be once you actually get started (and they become habits), but the rewards will be momentous.

“The Universe doesn’t give you what you ask for with your thoughts; it gives you what you demand with your actions.”

Dr. Steve Maraboli

BREAKING UNIVERSAL RESISTANCE

Breaking universal resistance is primarily about shaking up ruts or areas of stagnation. We are creatures that have an amazing capacity to ignore things that are not required at that moment — which is really helpful given how much stimuli we're bombarded with every day. We're not going to notice a painting that's been on our wall for years because it's not critical information to process at that moment. So we need to break out of this perceptual prison. Shake up the status quo. Take the dust off what's around us so we can evaluate what is working for us and what is working against us (there is no neutral); things you are indifferent about are an opportunity cost.

Again, you are in charge of what you pay attention to and what you want in your life. You must decide to get rid of all of the 'time and energy suckers' that have infiltrated your world because you didn't actively put up a firewall to keep them out. But once you make this effort, maintaining it is infinitely easier (and worth it). Remember: awareness is half the battle.

“Thinking will not overcome fear but action will.”

W. Clement Stone

CHANGE YOUR SCENERY

The quickest and easiest way to incite chaos, propulsion and momentum (and break up resistance) is to change your scenery. Changing your physical scenery is as easy as moving the art around to a different wall or moving your furniture. I once swapped my bedroom for the dining room because I wanted to wake up to the view. It was insanely liberating (and a ton of fun). Mind you, this was easier when I wasn't living with anyone but my dog, but I still have spaces to call my own that I can affect. If you don't, start by making space.

The idea is to shake things up. You can rearrange your furniture (the primary form of Feng Shui), paint your walls, get out of bed on the other side, take a different route to work or eat with your non-dominant hand. You don't have to do it for long, just long enough to reset your reliance on ruts and open up your peripheral vision. Pay attention to things you don't think about even a little bit and try to shake them up. As my friend Craig says, "Shaking things up exfoliates your brain," which I believe is the precursor to allowing new information in and changing old habits. This is the beauty (and the scary part) of embracing chaos, but it is essential to creating the space you need to allow change to happen.

"It doesn't have to be forever to be a good thing."

Lynette Xanders

MORPHIC FIELDS

We can all thank Rupert Sheldrake for this little bit of genius, but I'll oversimplify in the hope that the essence of it sticks. In a person, becoming obsessed with a thought can attract a thing (good or bad). Remember the skiing trees analogy? What you focus on brings it to you (and the Universe doesn't hear negatives). One of my friends said the only 'rule' he had in place when he started his ad agency was 'no law firms.' Well, he said it aloud and guess what made up the bulk of his client list before he actively cleaned house? You guessed it.

In groups of people, it can be a shared mindset or a topic you're discussing that gains voltage because of the collective energy around it. Ideas 'buzz' in some circles and not in others. Here's an old adage that demonstrates the power of this concept: if you have four rich friends, you're likely to be the fifth. If you have four poor friends, the same is true. What you surround yourself with, what you think about, what you write down and what you say out loud can determine an outcome. In short, it is the cultivation of 'the spirit of' something.

A vision board is an easy way to put your intentions into a form that becomes an anchor. This anchor wiggles its way into your subconscious and creates a morphic field around it, which in turn attracts that thing. Some have called this manifesting but I think that gives too much credit to the 'author' and not enough to the parts we don't yet understand. Either way, it should work even if you don't fully believe it. But once you believe it, you'll see it everywhere.

“You are what you surround yourself with.”

Lynette Xanders

FENG SHUI EVERYTHING

Feng Shui, simply put, is the design of +/- energy. The exact placement of furniture, elements and amulets will affect the amount and direction of energy flow. It's the act of moving things around and assigning intention that affects the energy you receive. You can Feng Shui a space by changing its physical design and decor that ultimately 'feels better' to you, even if you can't explain why.

With this same definition, you can Feng Shui your beliefs, your priorities, your friends, your job, your finances and your everyday thoughts and worries by cleaning them up, accepting or rejecting them, changing their priority and your desires around them and, thereby, their influence.

There are some rules around Feng Shui that you need to follow to achieve the benefits of physical redesign. I recommend buying Karen Rauch Carter's book, *Move Your Stuff, Change Your Life*, to get started.

Applying this philosophy to your life can start now. Simply pay attention to everything you surround yourself with and start making a decision about each – whether to keep and celebrate it, change it or let it go.

PHYSICAL FENG SHUI 101

Draw your office space, either at work or at home, outlining doors, walls and windows from a bird's eye view. Now redesign the layout by placing your desk so you are facing the door when seated (this is the 'seat of power'). Organize everything else accordingly.

FINANCIAL FENG SHUI

To make sure you haven't lost the point, I'll reiterate: just as you can Feng Shui a space, you can Feng Shui every aspect of your environment. The starting points of good fiscal Feng Shui are:

1. Clean out your wallet. A wallet that is breaking at the seams is riddled with clutter and is effectively stapled to the ground. Holding old receipts is symbolically an imprisonment in your past. Your primary wallet should only be for the cash and cards that you use regularly. If you have business cards, rewards cards, etc. filling up your space, get a second wallet for these. Now put your dollar bills facing the same direction (all should face forward and right side up). This is essentially showing respect to your money and it will, in turn, bring you more.

2. Know where it goes. Just like scraping together small bits of time to create an adequate window to get something substantial done, cut back on unnecessary **fiscal** fragmentation. For example, if you don't buy that latte every day or if you bring your lunch to work, you coul pay for a fabulous vacation. Or perhaps get out of debt. Know how much you need to cover your necessary bills and work back from there.

3. Give it away and it will come back to you three-fold. Nothing brings more money like giving it away because money is supposed to FLOW. Don't loan money, gift it. Tip well. Pay people who need the work to help you with things – everyone has to eat.

“Efficiency feeds flow and flow creates abundance.”

Lynette Xanders

CLEAR CLUTTER

Just as efficiency fuels creativity, clutter fuels stagnation. There are many forms of clutter although we usually focus on the physical form – junk drawers, piles of shoes by the door, piles of papers on the counter and our desks, old files in the cabinets, cabinets that are disheveled or full of expired items, clothes that are packed too tight, etc. Feels awful just thinking about them, I know. But it has to go. All of it.

Start with one thing that's small and manageable. Then focus on what you look at or are aware of every day, like the inside and outside of the front door. It's a double positive – you no longer feel the drag of resistance when you leave your house and you get a lift from seeing a clean, beautiful space when you return – it's a win, win.

Note that there are other forms of clutter aside from physical clutter that need to be addressed. Things left undone clutter our subconscious. Broken or unreliable things (appliances, cars, etc.) clutter our time in dealing with them. There's fiscal clutter (all the little things that nickel and dime our finances), electronic clutter (cords, desktop, big unused files) and even people clutter ('vampires' who fill your telephone time or break time with energy-sucking drama or negativity. You know who I'm talking about.) I can't tell you exactly how to break up with them, just that you need to be honest, be unavailable and/or be very clear about your boundaries. Take a day to tackle something and use the momentum to create more momentum.

WHERE TO BEGIN?

Write down, in order of importance, where you would start to eliminate clutter:

"Begin at the beginning and go on til you get to the end; then stop."

(The King, Alice in Wonderland)
Lewis Carroll

CULTIVATE EFFICIENCY

On the opposite end of clutter is efficiency. Efficiency developed through organization of time and things. Now here's the good news. I was perhaps the most unorganized person I knew when I got this idea planted in my head, and it changed everything for me. In short: organization is a habit that can be learned, nurtured and cultivated by studying about it and practicing it (like exercising a muscle).

I used to think embracing organization signaled (and invited) a militant air — a lack of creativity and fun — that would overtake the free-spirited sensibilities that I was trying to nurture. I didn't like what it said about me, or felt to me, because I didn't see a benefit in it. I didn't think I was 'born that way.' But Stan Richards changed my view by explaining that efficiency does not kill creativity, it fuels it.

If time (and more importantly, energy) is saved by not spending it on the things that don't matter (e.g., unnecessary meetings) and redirected to the things that do matter (problem solving, ideation, creation and nurturing beauty, imagination and inspiration) you'll get where you want to go and you'll be far happier in the process. It is not an accident that The Richards Group is still the most creative and most efficient culture I've ever seen — with employees staying for decades in an industry that sees ridiculously high turnover. I now know that efficiency and happiness can go hand and hand.

NAME THAT INEFFICIENCY

What areas need to be tidied up in terms of the time and energy that seem wasted?

PRACTICE EFFICIENCY DAILY

Many successful people (especially entrepreneurs and innovators) make a daily practice of cultivating efficiency. They get the things that don't matter out of the way in order to focus on the things that do matter. They prepare ahead of time in order to avoid any last minute drama by 'getting their ducks in a row.'

I know I've said this before but I want to make sure you are listening. Find ways every day to make things easy on yourself later. As my friend Ben said to me, "You work really hard at making things really easy." This is how you get out of the spiral of daily fillers that get in the way of your happiness.

My evening ritual, to prepare for the next day and to set the stage for a Zen morning, is to: Fill the gas tank so I don't have to stop on my way. Set up the coffee maker so all I have to do is 'press play,' pour and go. Prep my lunch. Check the weather and lay out my clothes. Print materials needed for the day. Set my keys and shoes where I can find them.

Some people have called this 'parking on the downhill slope' and once you make prepping a habit, the positive effects will snowball and leave you delicious windows of time and energy to make something beautiful and important. It's the thrust you need to change the dynamic from being reactive to being proactive in every aspect of your life.

“Never commit to memory what you can look up.”

Lynette’s Dad (Gatorade Birther)

CREATE SYSTEMS

Creating systems results in a chain of events that leads to efficiency. The rule for systems is the same as the rule for tool management, decorating and moving: keep like things together. For example, establishing space and rituals around paying bills includes everything from deciding where your mail goes when it comes in, to setting a schedule and reminders, to setting up bill pay or having your balanced checkbook at the ready (with envelopes and stamps nearby) and to having a paper recycling station. Want to quickly find a Band Aid? Organize your medicine cabinet by grouping things by ailment (cuts, colds, etc.). Organize kitchen drawers by putting all of the 'cutting' things in one and 'stirring' things in another. You can create a system for anything; organize and watch your life fall into place.

My favorite system is centered around travel. Packing used to really stress me out and take more time than I wished, because I travel a lot and to different climates during one trip. So, I decluttered my closet by separating work clothes and play clothes. I changed all my hangers to the same type to save space and visual frenzy. I organized my clothes by fabric weight. I stacked clothes in drawers on their ends so I could see everything at a glance and didn't have to pull stuff up from the bottom. Now when I pack I go straight to work clothes and grab lightweight and heavier weight without having to sort through everything. I also have a separate kit of toiletries that is always at the ready so I don't have to redo it every time. Makes a weekend get away much more likely to happen, too.

SYSTEM ID

What systems could you put in place that would save you time and/or stress?

INVESTIGATE WHAT YOU WANT MORE OF

Once I got the bug to learn how to organize, I did what I do for all of my clients: I researched it. I am still a perpetual student of efficiency — trolling books, magazine articles (everything from Harvard Business Review to Real Simple, YouTube, etc.) — because one little change can reap huge rewards.

The power of investigation started when I was in my mid-30's. I found a dream house and didn't want to wait to meet my life partner so I set off on my own to buy it. I was making good money, but houses were (and still are) crazy expensive in the NW and I didn't think I could afford one. My dear friend K. sat me down and did my first budget. She explained very simply that I could afford the house if I stopped eating out every meal. I explained very simply that I didn't know how to cook. In her lovely Southern twang she slapped me between the eyes with, "Girl, if you can read you can cook." I hadn't thought about it that way but it was an overwhelming thought (we now have Timothy Ferriss' book *The 4-hour Chef*). So she signed us up for a four-session power cooking class and we all lived happily ever after.

The most powerful help I received was through hiring a professional organizer (several times when I felt overwhelmed) and, in a weekend (for about $250), I leapfrogged a backlog and learned some new tricks.

When in doubt, ask a professional. This may seem obvious, but I'm amazed by how many people don't investigate what they want to learn and how long it took me to accept this strategy as a viable one. Whether or not you hire a professional, definitely invest in a few books on a subject that interests you. Buying a book breaks the seal and can show you how to overcome resistance in several ways: it sets an intention, is an anchor for the idea, is an action and begins to create a morphic field. If you're a web surfer, capture ideas you find in one (physical) place by taking notes in a dedicated journal. Regardless of the form, the idea is the same: investigate a thing to get more of a thing.

"If you can read, you can cook."

Kristen Weaver Dardani

TOPICS TO INVESTIGATE

What skills could you learn (or master) that would help you get closer to your ideal?

LOSE DRAINS

As I have mentioned before, one of our gifts as humans is the ability to ignore things that irritate us. Just as an oyster makes a pearl from a grain of sand that would otherwise cause endless irritation, we tune out those things (at least to some degree) that get in the way of our energy flow. The problem is that we ignore or accept these drains instead of dealing with them. What I've found from talking to people about their drains is that a great many of them can be greatly reduced, if not eliminated. And while most tell me that it's 'impossible' to tackle these drains, it's actually entirely possible although perhaps a bit inconvenient or uncomfortable. The question becomes, how badly do you want it (to be happy)? What happens if you can make your drains go away? What happens if you don't?

In order to lose drains, we have to be aware of them. We have to take inventory of those things that cause us irritation or drain our energy. You should have already audited your drains, but if you haven't, do it now. And remember to please write them down because it keeps them from flying around in your head. List all of the people, places and things that bring you down (at home and at work). Sometimes they're little things, sometimes they're big things but I often find that big things are little and little things are big. For instance, invoicing and taxes drove me crazy, so I hired a Director of Sanity via CraigsList to help me out. Identify it, then find a way around it — it's as simple as that.

I've spent many years helping creative companies optimize their culture and, in doing so, I find that a few small changes can vastly improve the collective energy (productivity, happiness and morale).

A while back I worked with an agency that was suffering from issues that ended up stunting their growth, financially and culturally. I discovered that the designers were drained by mismatched forks in the lunchroom (they're all about aesthetics you know). A $20 trip to Ross to buy matching sets solved that problem in under an hour. Other employees were drained by negative attitudes and language that dominated conversations, so I put hotel bells on conference room tables. Every time they heard the bell ring, they had to reframe, reset or restate what they said – thus completely changing their behavior and bad habits. These two changes were part of a recalibration that led to this company making more money in the year following this work than in the previous 10 years combined. The churn (losing good employees and clients) stopped. Growth was restored.

Many people I've had in workshops are pulled down by the words, actions and/or attitudes of outside forces (most often a dog or kid that is making them feel totally out of control). My advice is almost always to start with investigating how others have resolved these issues (e.g., Cesar Milan and Supernanny use the same framework). Earlier, you took a pass at reducing your drains but this is your chance to do it in earnest. Don't forget that 'call a professional' counts (if you really do it). As I've been told since I was a tot: "Do something, even if it's wrong. It's later than you think."

Draining Drains

Write down the steps you will take to reduce or remove your key drains:

GET OFF THE TREADMILL OF EXPECTATIONS

These are the 'I need to' lists that are often the source of a great deal of angst. Mostly among women and often surrounding Holidays, they often come from a place outside of our own making. In my world, as an example, I'd rather be playing than cooking a huge meal, so I go out to eat on Holidays. Sending cards every year is a drain, so I gave myself permission to not send them out each year. One year, my sister did them for me as a gift and voila – I'm on the every-third-year-program which really helps me enjoy the Holidays more. In looking at your drains, don't just accept that things have to be there just because everyone's doing them. It's your life and only YOU are in charge of your happiness.

In the work environment, there are a lot of expectations (self-imposed or stated) like picking up the phone right away or answering an email within the hour. I have rarely seen these stated, by the way, unless you're on a deadline. Most people feel like they have to because they can – or more often, they're avoiding other kinds of work. If you defrag your schedule, as suggested earlier, you'll need to let go of this instant response mechanism.

Here are few ways you can wean yourself from these habits:

1. Pretend you are on an airplane (pre-wifi enabled, like in the good old days) or at a conference.

2. Turn off the 'bells' or close your email.

3. Do your thinking and writing away from your desk to avoid interruptions.

The sky won't fall. The work will still get done, I promise. And it will likely be BETTER work. You need to begin to define success by the quality of your outputs and not by filling your days treading water. And if you break these habits – you will have more time to handle the big stuff and it will make you exceedingly happy.

RESET EXPECTATIONS

What three 'expectations' could you reset that would make your life better/happier/easier?

“Just because everyone’s doing it doesn’t make it right. And just because no one else is doing it doesn’t make it wrong.”

Lynette Xanders

DESIGNING IS ATTACHING VALUE TO THINGS

Remember that meetings were one of my key drains? I couldn't really have a rockin' plan b for these types of things but it helped to change the way I thought about them and managed them. So here's where designing things came in. I decided that having a meeting in a dreary room with no fresh air and lots of brown and plastic cups should cost more than a meeting over food and wine in a lovely spot...because those are conversations and the former costs me more than the latter in energy and recuperation time. Now, I charge for meetings but I don't charge for conversations. I have lots of conversations with clients and potential clients which keeps my business humming and my happy meter at a nine. Even if I have a meeting in a gross environment, charging a premium for that time makes it worth it.

The idea is that every hour, every opportunity, every activity is not worth the same. It's a bit like Chutes and Ladders. Some squares/activities are worth more (or cost you more) than other squares. They expand and contract (like a slinky). It's not that you want to protect yourself completely from all drains, just know that what you're getting paid, or the rewards, should be commensurate with what it costs you energetically.

A different perspective is illustrated by a friend who, by her own words, tried to maintain control and order in her household. She had an imaginative child and worked full time while trying to create a non-profit. Not a lot of time left in the day to color outside the lines. So I had her write down one of my favorite reset phrases, "What would the French do?" and keep it where she could see it regularly. We met again some time later at the most glorious lobby bar in Portland (the Urban Farmer in the Nines Hotel – everyone should spend time in spaces like these – but I digress). She said this quote helped her lighten up a little. And eventually, her son threw this line at her while trying to convince her that breakfast for dinner, out on the patio, was worth the effort. She relented. The kid is a genius. It could be as simple as having wine with lunch or having coffee in the bath or having breakfast for dinner. It is our choice to give ourselves permission to play.

What is this life if we defer enjoyment for some undefined time in the future? We need to incorporate at least a part of it now, whenever we can. Check out Timothy Ferriss' book, *The 4-Hour Workweek*, about the strategy of taking things on for three weeks that you're postponing until retirement. Brilliant. If it gives you energy and lifts your happy meter, it's worth it.

RE-VALUE YOUR DRAINS

Look back at the drains that you can't remove because they feed you in some way. They likely cost you energetically or they wouldn't be drains. For example, meetings are necessary for my business but I can't cut them out completely because they physically feed me, but they also drain me. What drains can you reconfigure to make them easier to swallow?

“Life is what you make it. Always has been. Always will be.”

Pearl Buck

MANTRAS

The use of quotes can be a great anchor to keep a goal or an ask 'in mind.' They remind us of what we love about our own view of the world and include a little bit of an 'ask' into what we'd like more of. I call these 'life quotes.'

You can have more than one, but the idea is to embrace one at a time. If you outgrow one, find another. I find writing them out longhand staples them to your thoughts — and can transform your actions.

Look for quotes that capture your higher order philosophy (that is always good to be reminded of). Ideally, they can be combined with what you want to reinforce in yourself or ask for more of (courage, confidence, balance, joyfulness, adventure). My one guardrail would be to make sure it's directed towards YOU. It has to be personal — it's not about other people. So while the 'do unto others' sentiments are noble, they have no business here. These are givens. You are a good person. It's about asking for what you need to become a great person. Say it with me: "It's all about me." At least for this moment. You'll know it's right by how it feels.

MORE OF MY FAVORITE QUOTES:

"When one door of happiness closes, another opens; but often we look so long at the closed door that we do not see the one which has been opened for us." - Helen Keller

"Live the life you love. Love the life you live." -Bob Marley

"If it isn't fun, you're doing it wrong." -Groucho Marx

"If you ain't just a little bit scared, you ain't driving fast enough." -Richard (King) Petty

"I've been through some terrible things in my life, some of which actually happened."

-Mark Twain

"Showing up is 80% of life." -Woody Allen

"Judge your success by what you had to give up in order to get it." -Dalai Lama XIV

FIND ONE THAT FITS

Google 'quotes' on a topic that interests you and write down the quotes that speak to you (and that you'd like to remember):

“I quote others only in order the better to express myself.”

Michel de Montaigne

CULTIVATE INSPIRATIONS

Do you have a clear idea of the people, places and things that lift you up and make your heart sing? Do you spend time regularly enjoying them? If you're like most, it's not likely. If you made a list earlier of lifts, awesome. If you didn't, do so now. What inexpensive, easy things can you do to lift your spirits? Light a candle? Walk the dog? Take a bath? Read an inspirational quote? Color? Visit an art museum or stationery store? Keep a list of these things in your calendar and instead of letting time between appointments fill themselves up, schedule them into your life. I repeat this because you'll need to revisit this idea after each wave of creating wiggle. Fill the spaces with good things.

If you love looking at antiques, for example, but can't fit it into a workday, try tapping Pinterest or Google images for a troll through things that might otherwise inspire you at an antique store. If you make your inspirations part of your rituals and space, you're even farther ahead of the game but, in the end, it comes down to how you're spending your time and energy. Make sure at least some of it is giving back to you every day (Stephen Covey's *Sharpen the Saw* is a good next read on this one).

Scaring yourself (or pushing yourself) can also help you find inspirations you didn't know were there. Seek goosebumps in every form to awaken your senses.

ADD MORE LIFTS

What more can you do to add inspirational people, places and/or things to your day?

"Do one thing every day that scares you."

Eleanor Roosevelt

BORROW ENERGY

This is great justification for a boondoggle (work that feels like play). The basic concept is that you can pull the positive energy from something that lifts you up while you're doing something un-fun that you can't lose or reduce. For example, if I have to get my papers together for taxes, I open the nicest bottle of wine I have in the house. If I'm trying to sort out a client problem, I'll take it with me skiing (the problem, not the wine).

Conventional (so-called) wisdom might tell you that the negative would ruin the positive, but I find the opposite is true. Granted, you might not enjoy that wine as much as you would sitting in front of a fire doing nothing, but it's worth it to make the tax prep job suck less. And I've yet to come off the mountain without a solution because I've given my subconscious time and space to sort out a problem by doing something else that's fun. If I need to think and write, I'll find a place that lifts me up and allows me to borrow its energy (often a hotel lobby or a restaurant with a white tablecloth). With gorgeous pen and paper as well, naturally. This gets me amped for the task and elevates my thinking. Conversely, if I try to sit in front of a computer or at the kitchen table with the same task, it becomes much harder and the outcome is often commensurate with the environment. It's an added kick of the good stuff that infuses your problem-solving capacity with positive energy.

LIVE ARTFULLY

A similar concept to borrowing energy but on a physical scale, my advice is 'use your good stuff.' Nearly everyone I talk to about this has a stash of good sheets, towels, glassware, etc. that they're 'saving.' Most often, they're saving it for other people (guests). You will get great energy from surrounding yourself with things that inspire you or make you feel worthy. While you may not think that using your nicest glass for your morning orange juice will do this for you, I beg to differ. At least try it for a month. Use your best stuff. Pull out a gorgeous pen and pad of paper instead of the spiral bound notebook and lint covered pen you're trying to get the last bits out of. See if it changes how you feel and think.

I believe that your mindset and environment can be cultivated and that it will spill out into your thoughts, your words and, ultimately, your actions. The thought here is a bit of 'fake it til you make it,' but more importantly, it's 'live in the now.' Erma Bombeck wrote a story a long time ago that really hit me. In essence, she put her favorite candle in storage and it melted. She never got to enjoy it. It may be one of the greatest tragedies of having too many options and too much stuff. If you surround yourself with only the things that you love, what would that do for you? Feng Shui experts say it would change your world, but I'll let you decide that. I just think it's way more fun and why not start there?

GIVE YOURSELF PERMISSION

What could you bring into your life that would add beauty or joy?

“If you never did you should. These things are fun and fun is good.”

Dr. Seuss

MASTER THE ART OF PADDLING

One of the greatest luxuries of our time, I believe, is deciding what we want to do (and doing it) in the moment. We are so pre-planned, scheduled and reactive, we rarely leave ourselves the time and space to 'paddle' (my word for paddling around the house barefoot, in pajamas, without plans). If you can give yourself a few hours or even a day to do this, you may catch the bug and require it every now and then to get back to yourself. I think this idea all started after reading Richard Brautigan's *Karma Repair Kit*, which, in essence, suggests we need to fully satisfy our physical needs for food and sleep and then shut out all noise in order to "arrive at the silence of yourself."

Paddling is this idea on steroids. Sleep until you wake up without an alarm. Then eat what you feel like eating, when you feel like eating it. Then go where the wind takes you. If you feel like cleaning out a drawer, then do it, but accept that you may just be distracting yourself. Have pen and paper and paints handy to capture thoughts (or they'll stop coming – you're channeling your inner voice). Do what makes you happy in that moment without listening or caring about what others want to do, eat or talk about. The trick is to forge a path between feeling what will fill your inner needs and addressing them in that moment. A day of paddling for me often equates to the same feeling I get after two weeks of vacation and the wise words that echo in my ears are worth it all.

“One cannot think well, love well, sleep well if one has not dined well.”

Virginia Woolf

EXERCISE YOUR CREATIVE THINKING MUSCLE

This one also bears repeating. It takes practice. Once we get the thoughts flowing, the next big thing is to put words to things...and ideally the RIGHT word. It is this practice that forges a path between what we see in our minds' eye and what we express to others. What we express to others creates the conditions for Providence (the universal conspiracy to help us get what we want).

Practice doesn't have to be painful – it just needs to become a habit. Name a color you see in nature – is it really just blue or is it cyan, cornflower or cobalt? Ponder thoughts like 'If Pluto is a dog, then what is Goofy?' or 'Is white chocolate decaffeinated?' Reverse it to find a visual representation of words – hit Google images and see what you think works best as an example of 'sassy' and 'saucy.' Try drawing something rather than explaining it in words. These are muscles that will help ideas form and help you articulate these ideas to yourself first and then to others. It should pinch a little at first, but then you'll start looking for the pinch.

FIND JUICY, EXTRAORDINARY WORDS

Many words people start with are blunt instruments. The eight-color crayon box, if you will, instead of the 64-color box. Practice renaming a nail polish color (**in extraordinary words**):

Ordinary Name		Extraordinary Name
Red nail polish	———>	"I'm not really a waitress" OPI
Grey nail polish	———>	"Haven't the foggiest" OPI
Grey crayon	———>	"Timberwolf" Crayon 64

“Think twice before you speak, because your words and influence will plant the seed of either success or failure in the mind of another.”

Napoleon Hill

FIND AN ANCHOR

One of the biggest hurdles to creating change is reminding yourself to do the new thing instead of the old thing until the new thing replaces the old thing. Some say it takes 21 days to create a new habit and that sounds reasonable to me. This is about how to remind yourself of where you want to go during this time. Yes, you should put lifts in your calendar to remind you. Yes, you should put quotes on your screensaver or bathroom mirror to plant the seed regularly. Yes, hotel bells can rally the troops around a commitment you've made to change. But you also need a more physical and personal reminder to get where you're going. This is about creating or augmenting your personal brand: how you see yourself and how you want others to see you that encapsulates and celebrates your new self (created through reaching your goals). I call this finding anchors.

A quick story to give you some context. When I worked at my first agency, I was essentially a consumer researcher. But I hated (and still do) the moniker of researcher (no slag intended, I just felt it was too 'backroom' for the impact I wanted to have). I really wanted to be in the creative department (mostly because they could wear jeans to meetings but I'll call it a calling). How did I transform my 'research' brand into a 'creative' brand? First I had to believe it myself. I had to feel it. I had to remind myself daily so that it would come through in my expressions (outputs that others could see – like the presentations I wrote and gave). My early experiments included painting my toenails electric blue so that when I took a shower in the morning I reminded myself of my goal.

Then I started wearing thumb rings to remind myself, when I sat down to write anything, to be more of my creative self than my research self. Eventually it led to wearing jeans to meetings (not at the same agency), but my evil plan worked.

The next time I actively set out to change my course (by going freelance), I needed to find an anchor to help me through the hard bits (namely the fear of doing it, which showed up at the end of every month when bills came due). I needed a physical expression to anchor the goal I set out (that would do double duty in being an anchor for my brand). To find this anchor, I started writing about what I offered clients that they would find valuable and what success in this capacity would look like. I also started paying attention to things that spoke to me. My symbol had to encompass both of these things to do what I needed it to do.

After some investigation, I realized I had painted and collected several 'suns.' At first I had no idea what I was trying to tell myself. So I applied what I had written to a sun symbol. Lo and behold, the sun captured what I thought I offered (illumination) and what I wanted (to live on a beach happily paddling out to the mailbox to collect money). This was the first placeholder logo for my business. I started building a brand around it by building a story around it. I tattooed a sun on my foot to remind myself (again, in the shower in the morning or bath at night) why I was working so hard instead of feeding my Netflix addiction.

WHAT IS YOUR ANCHOR?

What do you dream about? Doodle a symbol (use the following symbol chart as a starting point) that reminds you of what you want more of. When you're ready, you can look for a symbol that represents what you have to offer the world and what you'll get out of it if you do.

GROWTH
EFFICIENCY
ILLUMINATION
GROUNDED
PROTECTION
UNITY OF MALE + FEMALE
WISDOM
BALANCE
GOLDEN MEAN
STABILITY
FOCUS
ABUNDANCE
ENLIGHTENMENT
PURITY
OPPORTUNITY
SPACE
ALIGNMENT
MOMENTUM
VICTORY
SPIRIT
BELONGING
CHAOS
MASTERY
POWER
INSPIRATION
INTENTION
ENERGY
REFLECTION
INTUITION
CATALYST

ELEVATE YOUR BUBBLE

This is also worth repeating: generating creative momentum is not a 'one and done' endeavor. At the very least it needs a quarterly refresh — are you on track? Is that where you still want to go? What still needs more attention?

When you sit down to evaluate (it will take far less time in subsequent reviews), plan the time. Try paddling right before you sit down to write about it or review your lifts and drains. Track what has changed for the better. Pay attention to what's working and not just what's not. Give yourself permission to audit all of it and consider changing things you think you cannot change. Write and review in the morning, or leave your office and sit down with a glass of something nummy in a place that inspires you. This is your life.

Remember that you're not alone in this. Once you get clarity, drop your sandbags through alignment, and put changes into action, you will incite Providence (which again is the Universal conspiracy to help you get what you want). The quote on the following page is a concept that has been around for ages but somehow forgotten. It encapsulates the essence of what I've tried to lay out for you in this book much more eloquently than I ever could, but my hope is that you'll take it to heart. You have the power to do anything you want to do — so long as you commit to it. Just please remember to use your powers for good.

PROVIDENCE

"Until one is committed, there is hesitancy, the chance to draw back, always ineffectiveness. Concerning all acts of initiative (and creation), there is one elementary truth that ignorance of which kills countless ideas and splendid plans: that the moment one definitely commits oneself, then Providence moves too. All sorts of things occur to help one that would never otherwise have occurred.

A whole stream of events issues from the decision, raising in one's favor all manner of unforeseen incidents and meetings and material assistance, which no man could have dreamed would have come his way. Whatever you can do, or dream you can do, begin it. Boldness has genius, power, and magic in it. Begin it now."

William Hutchison Murray

THANKS

This book would not have been possible without several key people: primarily my parents, who gave me great, albeit unusual, advice (like focusing on getting A's in speech and typing because it's what would serve me best and spending all of my other energy having a good time because it would last me longer). You guys rock. My thanks also to my husband, who makes me belly laugh every day, encourages me to ski even though I have far too much to do and who reminds me that talking about it is not the same as doing it. To the CT's, who not only encouraged me to write this, they broke the seal. And finally to my very talented and generous friends, HV and KM, who spent many a weekend helping me do this because it was important to me. May every good thing in the world come your way.

READING LIST

Here are just a few of the many books that have influenced my thinking and my life:

The War of Art	Steven Pressfield
The 4-Hour Workweek	Timothy Ferriss
The Art of Looking Sideways	Alan Fletcher
The Red Rubber Ball	Kevin Carroll
The Alchemist	Paulo Coelho
The Happiness Project	Gretchen Rubin
Finding Your Own North Star	Martha Beck
Think and Grow Rich	Napoleon Hill
Creating Wealth	Robert Allen
The Artist's Way	Julia Cameron
The Life Changing Magic of Tidying Up	Marie Kondo
Move Your Stuff, Change Your Life	Karen Rauch Carter
You are a Badass	Jen Sincero

Enjoy the ride and keep me posted.

Lynette Xanders is the CEO and Chief Strategist of Wild Alchemy, an insight-based brand strategy, creative development and cultural momentum company designed to optimize and create something amazing[SM].

20+ years at advertising agencies such as Cole&Weber, DDB Seattle, BFS/Chiat Day, BBDO Vancouver and The Richards Group, 20 years at Wild Alchemy's helm, and as an external partner for some of the best agencies in North America, Lynette has a richly diverse client and category experience base.

Clients and projects span large, global brands such as Nestlé, E&J Gallo, Nike, SONOS, Miller Beer, Cadillac, Microsoft, LucasArts, Wyndham, and Virgin to smaller NW gems such as Amtrak Cascades, Salt & Straw, Umpqua, Nordstrom, Doc Martens, Rejuvenation, Deschutes Brewery, Devine Paints, Coffee People and Outward Bound. A full client list is available at wildalchemy.com.

In addition to being an experienced moderator and brand strategist, Lynette conducts training workshops for agencies, design firms and companies like Patagonia, Columbia and Adidas' Global Innovation Team. Find out more at wildalchemy.com. She and her family live in Sisters, Oregon to appease their skiing and elbow-room problem.

To learn more about speaking engagements, books and workshops, go to: lynettexanders.com or wildalchemy.com.

ISBN 978-0-9825623-2-1

Designed by Hever Velázquez
Edited and Produced by Kathy Middleton